Making Money With Mini Storage Auctions

Real Insider Tips And Tricks

by C.E. Williams

Copyright Notice

Copyright © Vampa Media Productions 2011. All rights reserved. None of the materials in this publication may be used, reproduced or transmitted, in whole or in part, in any form or by any means, electronic or mechanical, including photocopying, recording or the use of any information storage and retrieval system, without permission in writing from the publisher. To request such permission and for further inquiries, contact Vampa Media Productions at contact@vampamedia.com.

First Edition: 2011

ISBN 978-1463596484

Trademark Disclaimer

Product names, logos, brands, URLs, web site links, and other trademarks featured or referred to within this publication or within any supplemental or related materials are the property of their respective trademark holders. These trademark holders are not affiliated with the author or publisher and the trademark holders do not sponsor or endorse our materials.

Copyright Acknowledgement

Photographs attributed to a third party are the property of such third party and are used here by permission. All such attributed photographs are subject to the copyright claims of each respective owner.

Legal Disclaimer
Although the author and the publisher believe that the included information is accurate and useful, nothing contained in this publication can be considered professional advice on any legal or accounting matter. You must consult a licensed attorney or accountant if you want professional advice that is appropriate to your particular situation.

I first heard about storage auctions when I was growing up, years ago, and the idea has always held both mystery and appeal. Since then, storage auctions have become quite popular through cable reality shows that deal with the subject. I decided that I wanted to write a simple, no-nonsense guide, based on my experience for those who wanted to get into the fun. This is that guide.

I have been to quite a few storage auctions and I have had a lot of fun doing it. You never know what you are going to find in all those boxes. Anything is possible. I have found money, jewelry, guns, antiques and collectibles in units that I have won. I have also found more household items than could be imagined. Storage auctioneers are a lot like fisherman and they love to tell stories about what they caught and the one that got away too. I have heard plenty of stories to tantalize about finding safes full of gold and cash as well as people having gotten rich from buying an overlooked celebrities forgotten storage unit. There is both fun and money to be had, and I have had plenty of both, I can promise you fun at the very least.

Now, before you go and quit your job, you should understand that there is a learning curve to hitting the storage unit auctions and you are going to have ups and downs. I won't lie, I have bought units that were full of junk and I could have kicked myself. However, if you give it time, treat it as a hobby at first, you will find that your expertise and profits will both grow quickly.

Why Auctions Happen

One thing I want to discuss before we dive into anything is why auctions happen. A lot of the time when I first start talking about storage auctions, people look at me like I am some kind of a vulture or ghoul. Some people, who haven't thought about things, seem to think I am profiting on the misfortune of others. Let's get it all out on the table right away.

The only reason that a person's storage unit is foreclosed on is that they do not pay their bill. There are many, many reasons that someone might not pay their bill. They may not have the money, they may have died, they may have forgotten about the unit (this does happen and cost a celebrity big money), divorce can also play a part. Honestly, it could be any reason under the sun, but the simple fact of the matter is that the bill wasn't paid.

All those misfortunes that I listed may have made you a little uneasy. Well, let me tell you something that will make you feel better. Storage companies do not want to foreclose on a unit and avoid it at all costs. In most cases, the money that they recoup from an auction is nowhere near the amount of money that they are owed by the tenant. Also, a foreclosure ends the rental contract and a paying tenant is always much better than a paying auction winner. Because of all this, storage companies work very hard to get into contact with the tenant, and try to work things out before the unit is put up for auction. An auction is always a last resort. In most cases, no one has been able to reach the tenant in months and the property can safely be considered abandoned. If you find a $100 bill on the ground, you are going to assume that it is abandoned and pick it up. You don't give too much thought to the person who lost it. This is pretty much the same case.

Getting Started

Before you go fishing and have lots of fun, you need to go out and buy some gear. You can't do much fishing without a pole. Storage auctions are the same thing. You are going to need to buy some gear before you get started. Don't worry, it won't cost you a lot to get set and you won't need to take out a loan.

A good solid flashlight is the first thing you are going to need. I laugh every time I am a an auction and I see some new auctioneer show up without one of these. I never can understand how they think they are going to see anything. Now, don't go and buy just any flashlight. Don't go and bring a freebie LED light that is powered by 3 AAA batteries. Those are great, but totally inadequate for what you are planning to use them for. You should spend a couple of bucks and make sure that you get a quality light. The type of light that I recommend getting is a high powered, 1,000,000 candle power, LED spot light. You can find these in any hardware area of any major retailer. They should cost you about $25 bucks or so. Make sure you charge up the light before you go to the auction. I have seen people take them out of the plastic right there at the action and then be surprised that they only last 10 minutes. You need to do a little planning ahead, or people are going to laugh at you.

You are also going to need to bring some locks with you. If you win an auction, you are going to be expected to be able to lock the unit up immediately. After all, you are now the new legal tenant. If you are not able to lock the unit immediately, some auctioneers will declare that you are not the winner and return the unit to bidding.

I like to take four locks with me. This is generally enough to take care of anything that I buy. If I buy any more than that, I know my garage will be overflowing and I know my wife will be cranky with me. Four helps to limit me to realty. I would recommend going out there and buying a four pack of locks that are keyed alike. This way you only have to carry one key around with you and you won't sound like a high school janitor walking through the halls. You can buy four packs of locks that are keyed alike, again, in the hardware section of any major retailer.

Beyond that, all you need to buy is a good pair of sturdy work gloves. In most cases, you should already have some of these. If you don't and you need to buy some, spend a little bit of money and get the thermal gloves (storage parks can be amazingly cold even in summer) with insulated rubber on the handprint. These are great for keeping your hands warm and for helping you keep a grip on whatever you are carrying.

If you go and buy these three items, you should have everything you need to start prospecting in storage units at your earliest convenience. However, there is one other thing you need. That's money.

Now, the amount of money that you take with you to a storage auction should be "fun money". I would be pretty irresponsible if I told you to go out and buy storage auctions with your rent money or your kid's tuition money. Look at this money like you would when you are at the blackjack table. You are having fun with it, but you can lose it if you play a bad hand. Storage auctions are like that too. You usually won't lose the money that you pay to buy a unit, but you can. I have bought a loser a time or two (I have bought winners considerably more often though).

So, take what you deem is appropriate. You don't need to bring a fortune with you either. I bought my first unit (a 10'x20') for under $100 and I see units sell for $1 all the time. Whatever you do decide to take with you, it is best to take it in cash. Some storage companies will accept credit and debit cards, but everyone will accept cash.

Now, with all your gear and cash set aside, you are ready to go out and find yourself some auctions and some treasures. But how do you do that?

Finding The Auctions

When I first started prospecting in storage units, the only place that you could find the auctions advertised was in the newspaper. These days, I don't even get a newspaper. As time has marched on, where you look for the auctions has changed too. One thing I will say, is that finding auctions is free and easy. I have seem websites that want to charge for the information. Don't bother with these, they just want your money and you can find the information on your own.

The first place that I like to look for auctions these days is still the newspaper companies, I just prefer to do it through their websites these days. You can usually scan the classified sections of your town's newspaper without ever leaving your couch. Look in the public notices sections. This is where the storage companies have to advertise foreclosed units in by law. In most cases, they must do this at least 30 days prior to the sale. I search on the weekends, usually, when I get home and I write down all the auctions that are coming up in the next few weeks. I have a little calendar planner that write everything down in. Although, these days, I see a lot more people writing everything down in their smartphones instead, I still like the pen.

The next place that I like to find auctions is through the storage companies themselves. Right now, in America, there is a boom in storage unit construction. Lots of people are having to downsize their housing and are needing space to store all their stuff. Even the big banks are investing in storage parks these days. Well, this is true in my area as much as anywhere else.

I keep my eyes open and as soon as I see a new storage park open, I go in and ask them when they plan to be having auctions. They are always very friendly and tell me when the next one is. Always ask if they have a calendar planned out in advance. If they do, ask them for a copy of it. This will give you a jump on things and can fill your schedule for the rest of the year.

A lot of storage companies do auctions on a regular basis. For example, auctions will be held on the third Thursday of the month. I love to find a company that does it like this. That way, I always know when they will have them and I can plan ahead.

The last place that I like to look for storage unit auctions is on the websites of the storage unit companies themselves. In my area there are several chains. When I first got into storage auctions, I figured out which company owned which parks and I found their company websites. You can usually search the company websites with the word "auction" to find what you are looking for. If you don't try a search engine search with something like "ANY TOWN STORAGE.COM auctions" and you should find what you are looking for. These are a great resource because they will usually have the full year listed in advance. Also, when companies have a lot of parks that need to do auctions, they will do progressive auctions and travel from site to site in one day. That means you can make a whole day out of auctions if you are inclined to do so. I will warn you in advance, there is no lunch break.

I would recommend that, when you are first starting out, that you limit yourself to within 20 miles or so of your home. A lot of new people overlook the work that is required to transport all your newly won treasures back to your house, or the inconvenience of driving 50 miles to meet a buyer at the unit you bought. Either way, you can always choose to move farther afield if you decide it's worth it.

Auction Day

First of all, if you can, try to go to the auction with a second person. This will be helpful for many reasons. A second set of eyes can see things that you may have missed. This happened to me once and the person I was with spotted a German WWII Luger pistol. It sold for $50 and was easily worth over $500. Also, a second person can help ground you to reality. I have experienced the euphoria of winning an auction before and sometimes you can lose your head in the fight. A second person will help you to keep prices and values in perspective.

Now, most auctions happen during the AM and they can start as early as 7 AM. So first and foremost, set an alarm. Also, you should plan on taking a thermos full of coffee with you too. This will help perk you up and help you keep warm. You should also always plan to be at an auction 30 minutes early. This is actually just a good policy for life in general, but it also helps at an auction.

On a side note, I love to go to storage auctions in the rain. This usually vastly decreases the number of bidders and by extensions, lowers the amount of money that I have to pay to get a unit. Get a good umbrella and suck it up. This can be a huge plus to you and your wallet.

You will usually need to fill out paperwork identifying who you are as a bidder. The storage companies are required to do this by law so they can prove that an auction happened and that they did not just keep the stuff for themselves. You will need to fill this paperwork out before the auction begins and the extra 30 minutes means you don't have to rush. This is also a good time to ask how many units are for auction. In most cases, the number that are for auction will be smaller than the number that was listed in the newspaper classifieds. People see that their unit is going up for auction and make an arrangement wit the storage company. This takes their unit out of the auction.

If this is your first time at an auction at this particular location, you should feel free to ask how the auction is conducted. In some cases there will be a professional auctioneer with a bullhorn and you hold up your hand when you agree to pay the price he is calling. Other auctions are informal and you just shout out the amount of money you are willing to pay. Some auctions are silent and you will write down the unit number and the amount of money you are willing to pay on a piece of paper that you turn in at the end of the auction. Either way, each location will have it's own rules and you should be familiar with these before the auction begins. Don't be afraid to ask questions. That's how you become a pro!

Another variation that you should ask about before the auction begins is what the terms of the auction are. In some cases, the units will be sold as whole lot. In essence, you are bidding on the whole contents of the unit. In other cases, you can find yourself in a piece auction. In a piece auction, the units are unloaded and each item is bid on individually. It varies by storage company. Whole unit auctions bring in less money for the storage company and guarantee that the unit is empty and ready to rent within a few days, whereas piece auctions mean the storage company has to pay someone to haul everything away. However, with a piece auction, the storage company usually brings in more money from the sale of items to offset that. Either way, its a business decision that you should be familiar with.

I also like to get to an auction 30 minutes early because it allows me to sit and listen to the competition. My hearing got very perceptive when I worked as a bartender and you will never believe what some people talk about before an auction. Some will describe what they are looking for or you can hear fun tips and tricks. You might also hear about good auctions that they have been to or are planning to go to in the near future. You are new at this, so the more you can learn the better. Listen and learn.

Once everyone has filled out their paperwork and the time for the auction, as was listed in the ad, the auction will begin.

In most cases, you will wind your way through the park from unit to unit. The auctioneer (usually the park manager) will open the unit and let everyone take a look. In my experience, park manager's are good at this. They will let everyone take a look and you don't need to crowd or push your way to the front. Generally, you will not be able to go into the unit and you will be limited to simply looking from the opening. In the case of a big unit like a 20'x20' this can really tell you very little. Instead, you have to rely on some tools, tricks and intuition to analyze the unit and decide if it is worth bidding on.

Well, the first tool that you have at your disposal is that trusty big flashlight that I told you to go buy. Well, feel free to shine that thing into every nook and cranny that you can see into and examine what it lights up. Take your time doing this and don't be rushed. Look carefully at everything that is lit up and figure out what it is if you can. Many times, I have looked patiently and methodically only to see something everyone else missed that makes the unit worth a lot of money. In one case, the item that I recognized, that no one else seemed to was worth $700 and I sold it by the end of the day. I had paid a mere $50 bucks for the unit that everyone else had thought worthless.

You should also look carefully at the bases of any boxes you see. These can give you some indications of what might be in there.

First, look and see if you see any wetness or stains on the bottoms of the boxes, like they had been exposed to flooding of any kind. If I see **ANY** indication of this, I will usually pass on a unit. It is not worth the time, trouble or headache of dealing with a bunch of mildewed and moldy junk. Do yourself a favor and follow the same rule.

Next, look at the boxes themselves. What are they from? Are they boxes from a big plasma TV or are they empty liquor boxes? This type of information can (but not necessarily) figure out the economic background of the person storing the stuff and can give you a clue to what might be in there. One tip I will pass on is to not go crazy because you see a big electronics or computer box. More often than not, these are empty boxes or are storing something else. This doesn't mean that you can't take it into consideration when you are bidding, but don't count your chickens before they are hatched.

Next, consider what you can see and what it might indicate is back there. If you see hunting gear, there could be guns of fishing equipment in the unit. Both are very valuable. If you see lots of computer cables and keyboards, there might be computers in the unit. If you see boxes and garbage bags full of clothes, the whole unit might be filled with clothes. If you see furniture and nicely, organized boxes, you could be looking at a whole household packed up in storage. Consider these connections carefully before you start bidding.

A valuable tip that I will pass on is to take a deep sniff of the unit. Storage unit buildings tend to be a cornucopia of smells (some bad). You need to make sure that what you are buying is not soaked in cat urine and mildew. If it is, I promise, you will not be able to sell it and you will not want it in your house. If you do buy a unit that is full of smelly junk, you will just have to break your back taking it all to the dump and you won't find any treasures or make any money in the process. So...take a deep sniff before you bid on anything.

One last tip I will offer is to just avoid some things. For some reason, soiled mattresses show up in storage auctions a lot. Don't even waste your time with them. They are worthless and you will just have to pay to get rid of them. Old computer monitors are another headache you should avoid if you can. They are loaded with mercury and antimony and you will have to pay hazardous chemical disposal fees to unload them. The same can be said for any chemicals or paints. Also keep an eye peeled for any chemistry glassware. This usually is a sign of a meth lab. This means all the stuff in the unit could be coated with nasty chemicals that you don't want to fool with. Again, just avoid the headache and steer clear in the first place. Trust your gut.

Once you have taken a good look and a good whiff of the contents of the storage unit, you need to decide if you want to bid or not. A lot of new auctioneers feel the need to bid on any old thing. I know when I bid on my first unit (which I won) I bit off a bit more than I could chew, but I was so excited to actually be bidding that I didn't care. Don't feel that you have to bid on every unit. However, if you feel that this one is right for you, by all means proceed.

The subject of auction bidding is not complicated, but it like everything has some finer points that you should familiarize yourself with to be good at.

First, I set a maximum amount which I will pay for a unit in my head. I never, ever go above this. This is just another one of those little safety measures that can keep my from getting wrapped up in the fun and excitement of the auction. After that, I start low. Always start with a lowball. Sometimes this has really helped me. For one reason or another the crowd is not interested in going after a unit in which I see some promise. Well, since I started with a lowball, I got the unit for a fraction of what I was willing to pay and thereby increased the profit I made by selling off the stuff inside of it. Move up in reasonable increments of $5 or $10. I hate the people who will just nickel and dime the auction and waste everyone's time by adding a measly buck to the bid. Do yourself a favor and don't be that person.

Lastly, stick to your guns and don't back down in the auction. Don't let other bidders intimidate you or push you around. You have as much right to be there and if you want what's in the unit, then bid until it's yours. I personally love a verbal auction. Nothing is sweeter than when you finally win and all the treasures are yours.

If you do win an auction, you will need to go pay for the unit. Don't do that right away if you are given the opportunity. Slap a lock on the unit you just won and keep up with the auction. One time, early on in my experience, I dropped back to secure some of he stuff I had just won. Well, I missed out on a unit I am still kicking myself for missing. Just like in elementary school field trips, always stay with the group. There will be plenty of time to explore your new treasures later!

When the auction is all over, you will need to pay for your units. Like I said before, cash is king at a storage auction. Once you have paid, you will normally be given no more than 48 hours to get all of the property out of the unit or you will be charged rent. If you have bought a bunch of units, or a big one, you can always talk to management and see if they can give you a little extra time. It never hurts to ask. The worse they can do is say no. If they are sticklers, you can always offer to pay them for a weeks rent or so. This usually has the effect that is needed.

Sorting Your Treasures

Once the auction is over, the fun part really begins. You get to go through and sort all of your treasures. I use the word treasure liberally in this document because going through a storage unit that you have bought at auction really is like finding buried treasure. You never know what you may come across.

The first decision that you need to make is whether or not you are going to sort your find where it is. That is to say, in the storage unit. I generally prefer to move everything to my garage so I have more time and tools at my disposal. However, there is nothing wrong with sorting everything in the unit if the management company has no problem with it.

If you choose to move all of your treasures you are going to need a suitable vehicle to do it. I have moved stuff with a minivan, a pickup truck and a rented moving van. Any one of these is plenty to haul whatever you need. Avoid renting anything if you can as it is just a cost that eats into any profit that you make.

If you have to rent anything, see if you can get away with renting a trailer. These tend to be cheaper than trucks. If you are going to be doing a lot of storage auctions, you may even give thought to purchasing a small utility trailer. There are many inexpensive trailers on the market that you can collapse and hang in your garage when it is not in use.

Once you have gotten your haul to an area where you can sort it at your leisure and are comfy, you get to start all the fun. Just dive in!

I generally sort into four piles. The first pile is stuff that I am keeping for myself. This is great. Anything you want is yours! I have taken clothes, tools, recreation gear, firearms, jewelry, electronics and furniture from storage units I have won. Many of the items are top quality and I paid next to nothing for them. The fact they were almost free makes me enjoy them even more.

The next pile of stuff are items that I can sell. These can be anything that is useable and in good condition. Think of this as a pile of stuff that you are salvaging from the dump. Don't worry about whether or not you can sell it at this point. Just identify an item as useable and move on from there. We will talk about ideas to sell your items in a just a bit.

The next pile is junk that needs to be disposed of. I say "disposed of" because not all of it needs to go to the local dump at your expense. This pile can include items that can be burned, like wooden pallets or damaged furniture. I have bought units with in which I found a ton of wooden pallets. Well, an hour with my trusty chainsaw (also from a storage auction) and they made for many lovely fires that winter.

"Disposed of" can also mean recycled. This includes metal which you can sell to local metal recyclers for a tidy amount of money. There are books available on the internet that can tell you everything you need about the finer points of metal recycling.

Chemicals are another item that can (and should be) recycled. This includes used car batteries, paints, finishes, automotive chemicals, solvents and fuels. You don't want these around in your garage as they can pose a safety risk. Cities and counties often offer hazardous waste recycling free of charge (so you don't dump it down the drain). For information on this, the best place to start is your local dump. They can tell you how to dispose of this material in your area.

Most likely, there will be a pile of stuff that needs to go to the dump. I would be very surprised if I didn't have to make a dump run when I was finished going through a storage unit. You are bound to find things that just need to go away. Boxes of porn and sex toys are common finds. These are of no use and go right to the dump.

One word of caution that I will make concerning the "Disposed of" pile is that you don't want to be to eager about throwing stuff on it. One time, I threw a box of hardware onto the pile of metal that was going to the recycler. They would have paid me, maybe, a few bucks for it. Well, for some reason, I took a closer look at it and realized that it was actually, a box of Victorian period door hardware. The pieces were even marked by the manufacturer. This was during the housing boom, so I took it to a dealer in the area that specialized in that type of thing. They gave me over $100 for the parts. I was just about to throw them away and the money with it. If you don't know what an item is, set it aside and do a little homework on it before you decide it's worthless and you can't be bothered with it. Actually the detective work can be fun too!

The last pile of stuff that I set aside are personal effect of the previous owners. In some states, you are required to do this by law. In others, it is performed as a courtesy to the former owners. Personally, I think you should do this, and do it well, just to be a good person.

Personal effects include business documents, photographs, family items, and the like. I generally will set up a box and just throw all this stuff into it. Frames, albums, file cabinets, etc. are not personal effect. You need to keep those. A painting is a judgement call. When you are done sorting the haul, you should return the personal effects to the storage company. They will then store them for a period of time in case the owner does turn up. However, their space is limited, as is their patience, so whittle the pile down to only items that are truly personal effects. Don't try to pawn off junk on the storage company. This will just get you a bad reputation.

Selling The Haul For Cash

Once you have sorted everything into piles and kept what you want, and disposed of what needed disposing, and returned the personal effects, you can sell whatever is left and usually turn a profit. Free stuff from a storage unit is great. Paying for a trip to Aruba with the profits from a storage auction is even better!

There are a lot of ways that you can sell stuff that you have found in storage auctions. I am definitely don't have a monopoly on good ideas and I will not claim that the list I am going to present here is exhaustive.

You do need to build up a bit of skill in finding out what an item is worth. Look for model numbers on anything you can to find out just what it is that you are dealing with. If you have model number, this will help you find items that are like it for sale. From there, you can gauge the price range of an item and where yours falls in terms of quality.

Books will have an ISBN and these are worth checking. I have bought a lot of used college textbooks and these can turn a profit surprisingly fast. That is, provided they have not been replaced by a newer addition. You can search by ISBN on any major book retailer's website. If you find that the book can be sold go ahead and sell it there. If not, remember that a book is paper and can be recycled.

I like to sell items online if I can. Internet ads really get the word out there quickly and cheaply and this makes it easy to get a good price in a timely manner. I prefer craigslist.org for items that are too big to ship such as furniture, appliances, yard equipment, musical instruments, etc. eBay.com is better for items that are small and can be shipped. Both of these will help you to move things quickly. For both you will need to set up an account. These are quick and easy processes.

Once you have your accounts set up you will need to post and ad. This is always better with a picture. Most people have a digital camera so just snap a few shots and load them up. You will be selling stuff before you know it.

If you are selling local, you need to figure out how you are going to conduct the sale. I have had people come to my house when I was selling large items like furniture, however, I am not in love with strangers tramping all over my yard. If I can I prefer to meet people in a public place like a mall or a grocery store and just do the sale there. Operate in your comfort zone, but you should have a plan before you need to come up with one on the fly.

If you have a gun, you cannot just sell it to anyone. They need to undergo a background check through the FBI at a licensed gun dealer called an FFL. Most pawn brokers are FFLs and will be happy to help you complete a sale. You can also find list of FFLs in your area through gunbroker.com. Gunbroker.com is an online gun marketplace and is another great place to sell any firearms that you come across. Just make sure you follow any and all applicable state and federal laws. If you are not sure, speak to a gun dealer in your area and seek his advice.

A garage sale is another really great way to turn the items you won at auction into cash in your pocket. This is also a great way to sell off mundane items like dishes, clothes, small appliances, furniture, tool, etc. You can easily advertise on telephone poles, with neighborhood signs, in the local newspaper or church bulletin and you are off and running. You don't need to be too fancy. Set up card tables if you want. I have made garage sale table out of sawhorses and plywood and no one seemed to mind.

Now a garage sale is really only an option when the weather is cooperative. If you live in the Southwest, this could be all year. In the North where I live, this window is much smaller. Plan accordingly. If you are buying units all year and plan to have just one garage sale in the summer, you are going to need to store everything until then.

If you don't feel like having a bunch of strangers all over your yard you can always consider selling your stuff at a rummage sale. A rummage sale is just a really big garage sale held by a church or charity in your area. There are also commercial rummage sales called "flea markets" that are an option. At flea markets you will need to pay for your table space, but this can often be more than made up for in the large amount of foot traffic that a flea market can generate.

If you decide that you don't want to store mundane household items all year waiting for a garage sale, there are two options to help get rid of this kind of stuff. The first is that you can bundle them and sell them cheaply online, or you can donate them. Either option has its benefits.

Bundling items household items like pots and pans is a great way to unload them. Someone is always moving out on their own for the first time and is in need of a pots and pan set. The same can be said of glasses, dishes, kitchen tools, hand tools, power tools, etc. Put together a big assortment of items that go together, charge a low, but reasonable price and you will usually sell them pretty quickly through craigslist.org.

Donating these same items is another great way to get rid of them ad can represent a tax write off for you in the long run. You will need to talk to your accountant about that one though. I am not a tax expert.

There are any number of charities out there that would be more than happy to take any unwanted household items on your hands. Some of them will even come to your house and haul them away for you at no cost to you. This is a win-win. The charities get items that they can sell through their second hand stores and you get the space in your garage back to fill with more treasures from storage units.

Sometimes, you are stuck with an item that you can't sell or donate. A perfect example is one of those soiled mattresses that I mentioned. Well, you can take them to the dump. This will eat up an afternoon and cost you some money. However, there is another step. You can give it away.

Sometimes an item that people will not pay for, will be fought over if it is being given away for free. I have done this a bunch of times. A stained mattress is perfectly fine to some people. I am always honest and upfront. Most people don't care and are happy when they drive away with a free mattress. Cathode ray computer monitors (the not flat screen type) are another example. They can still work fine and t saves people the money to buy one and you the trouble and money of recycling them. I once listed a broken down trailer I had for free and I had hundreds of eager people email me within 48 hours. Remember, one man's trash is really another man's treasure.

If you want to unload something by just giving it away, you can list it on the internet and put it in front of your house. I have done this a bunch of times and it is always one when I get home. No exceptions.

Final Thoughts

I hope this has been an informative and useful document for you and I wish you all the luck in the world of storage auctions. They are a fun way to spend time and make extra money. Good luck to you and happy hunting.

www.ingramcontent.com/pod-product-compliance
Lightning Source LLC
Chambersburg PA
CBHW021851170526
45157CB00006B/2402